My Sister's Keeper

Letters from the Heart for Pastors' Wives

Jeanne D. Wilson, Ed.D.

My Sister's Keeper

Copyright © 2010 by Jeanne D. Wilson, Ed.D.

All rights reserved. No part of this book may be reproduced or transmitted in any form or by any means without written permission of the author.

ISBN 978-1-4507-0345-1

Acknowledgments

I have grown tremendously from this spiritual journey and know that I could not have done it alone. I would first like to thank the women who contributed to this work:

Lady Genea S. Brice- Peoples Baptist Church
Oakland, California.

Lady Andrea Clark- Living Springs Ministry
Tracy, California.

Lady Denise Clark- Word Assembly Baptist Church
Oakland, California.

Lady Cindy Epps- Mt. Zion MBC
Cedar Rapids, Iowa.

Lady Florence Jones- Family Bible Fellowship
Newark, California.

Lady Rebecca Miller- Chosen Vessels Christian Church
Alameda, California.

Lady Stephenie Northington- Bethel Bible Fellowship
Oakland California.

Lady Mattie Washington-Abner- Revelation MBC
Berkeley, California .

Minister Cathy Bryant-Nelson-Revelation CF Singles Ministry Director.
San Leandro California.

I pray that God will continue to grant you wisdom and strengthen you.

To my sisters in Christ who blessed us with your story but wanted to remain anonymous...Thank you!

To my dad James E. Morgan and mom Jeannette C. Morgan thanks for the foundation of Christ and two separate homes filled with laughter and love.

To my babies Morgan and Kennedy thank you for praying for me every morning, "And Lord help mommy to finish her book and not get frustrated." From your lips to God's ears. May my spiritual and educational journey serve as a stepping stone for your own.

To my Revelation church family, thank you for your love, support and prayers. A special thank you to Vareece Jackson, my Armor Bearer Keisha Johnson, Cathy Nelson, advertising & marketing team Tawanna Smith and Rachel Simms and big Sis Ian Vaughn, who always made me feel that I could accomplish this goal even when I doubted myself.

Solomon Wilkins, thank you for guiding me step by step on how to publish and print my first book. You made what could have been an insurmountable task simple, and I am forever grateful. Looking forward to your two new books to be released!

Kim Huffman, Sherri Givans and Barbara Worthington, thank you for your meticulous and thoughtful edits/reviews of my countless revisions.

And last, but certainly not least, to my best friend in the whole world, my husband, Pastor Dwayne Wilson. A man who has shown me what real love feels like. Thank you for living the life that you preach and being my biggest supporter and encourager. You are the most loving, secure husband any woman could ask for.

Table of Contents

Chapter One: Why This Book Is Needed 1

Chapter Two: I Don't Want to be a Pastors Wife-A Cry for Help from a New Wife 5

Chapter Three: Who Am I? 11

Chapter Four: Remember Why He Married You 19

Chapter Five: Sit Down & Shut Up! Allowing Your Husband To Pastor Without All Your Opinions 23

Chapter Six: Don't Let Satan Use You! How Information You Tell Your Husband Can Be Detrimental to His Ministry 29

Chapter Seven: Do I Have to Go to Go to Church Again? Preventing Burn Out in Ministry 33

Chapter Eight: How 70's T.V. Shows Can Help You Be a Better Pastor's Wife 39

Chapter Nine: The Church as the Other Women...& Games Women Play: Keeping it Real with Old School Knowledge 47

Chapter Ten: First Ladies & Fasting 53

Chapter Eleven: Super Saint, Wonder Wife, Bible Believing Barbie – Balancing Ministry without Losing Yourself 56

Chapter Twelve: Is She Really After Man?........................ 61

Chapter Thirteen: I Quit-Life After Divorce..................... 65

Chapter Fourteen: Break Up to Make Up – Reconciled Marriages... 71

Chapter Fifteen: Show Her Your Love-Practical Advice for Pastors & Parishioners 77

Chapter Sixteen: How to Start Your Own Support Group 85

Chapter Seventeen: Practice Test: How Could YOU be Your Sister's Keeper?... 94

Chapter One:
Why This Book Is Needed

DR. JEANNE WILSON

To My Fellow Lady Laborers in Christ!

A pastor's wife is an ordinary woman in an extraordinary role! This book was written from the hearts of pastors wives who have been given the opportunity (notice I said opportunity and not challenge) to work in ministry alongside their husbands.

When a man accepts his "calling" to be a minister, it is one of the most significant, life changing moments he will ever experience. But this "calling" not only affects his life, but also will impact the life of his wife and family. His training could start at the seminary, where instructors begin to lay the foundation for his biblical understanding, or his pastor may take him under his wing, providing biblical and practical direction, but how will his wife be educated on her new role? How will she know what is required or expected of her? A study conducted on pastors revealed that most felt well equipped and prepared for their new role, in contrast to 85% of wives who did not. Although the qualifications can be left unspoken, the expectations can often be far greater than even those of her husband.

We are a group of women who have similar yet very unique experiences as current and former pastors' wives. These letters were written so that our sisters in Christ may have a better understanding of the essential role they play that can help or hinder their husbands in ministry. It is my sincere hope that these letters will provide support and guidance for the spiritual journey that lies ahead. Being a pastor's wife can be very rewarding, but it is extremely important that you do not lose your sense of self in the midst of trying to be everything to everyone.

It is no mistake that you picked up this book today. *My Sister's Keeper* is to be used as a tool to guide you towards embracing and accepting your purpose so that you will one day be able to encourage another sister to do the same.

In an effort to contribute to the physical, emotional and spiritual wholeness of a pastors/ministers wife, this book was also written so that the general congregation can have a fish bowl view into the life of this servant thereby gaining an enlightened understanding of the ambiguous position she holds.

We will start with a letter from a new pastor's wife expressing the feelings, emotions and questions she has when her husband acknowledges his "call" and is then asked to pastor a congregation.

The book includes letters from eleven wives who will answer her questions and many more, as well as give encouragement and insight about the sacrifices and struggles she will encounter as she strives to support her husband in ministry.

This book won't have all the answers but will try to point our sisters in Christ in the right direction with inspiration from GOD and personal life experiences, for we are our Sister's Keeper! Romans 12:10.

Jeanne D. Wilson, Ed.D.

Then the word of the LORD came unto
me, saying, Before I formed thee in the
belly I knew thee;
and before thou camest forth out of the
womb I sanctified thee,
and I ordained thee a prophet unto the
nations.

Jeremiah 1:4-5

Jeanne D. Wilson, Ed.D.

Chapter Two:
I Don't Want to be a Pastors Wife-A Cry for Help from a New Wife

ANNOYMOUS

I was raised in a home where my parents always battled religion. My mom being Catholic and raised by her grandmother who was white would always say, "Those fools (Baptist church folks) just want to jump and fall out on the floor all day." My dad, who was raised in Mississippi and is a Southern Baptist, would always comment on "those child molesters (Catholic church folk), "so I went to church when I felt like it because religion was never forced on me.

I met my husband while we were in high school, he grew up in church but when he graduated he did not attend service on a regular basis. As we reached our thirties, we decided for the sake of our kids we "might" need to start going to church more. We found a church that we both really liked, and even when I had to work he would still go to church and take the kids. I started to notice small changes; he didn't drink as much, didn't curse as much, he wasn't as mean.

A few years passed and he decided he wanted to go to theology school and learn more about God. Then he tells me about his *"calling."* It was really hard for me to accept. After all the things he put me through in our marriage, why would God call him of all people to preach? After a while I began to accept this "new husband." I was truly seeing a change, but it seemed that he went from one extreme to the other. He went from being a very "worldly" man, drinking, clubbing, womanizing to not drinking at all, reading the Bible all the time, going to school, needing quiet time to pray, and he was at church not just on Sunday's but almost every day of the week. At least when he was with other women I could act a fool. But now all his attention was going to the church, so I couldn't be mad, or I take that back, I (shouldn't) be mad, but I was.

About a year later, he visits another church with his grandfather, after which he comes home and says, "I preached today and God used me. This is truly my calling. They want me to come back!" My husband decided he wanted to join this new church but I was like, "Okay you can join, but God hasn't told me I need to change my church, so I'm going to wait on Him to tell me." I really didn't want to start over at a new church. I really liked my church and had made many new friends, something I don't do very easily. I spoke to my pastor's wife and she explained that although it would be a difficult transition I needed to be with my husband in ministry. I felt pulled so I went to visit my husband's "new" church not knowing how "traditional" this Baptist church really was. My first visit was on a 1st Sunday and I had on all black. Lord have mercy the looks I got! "The new minister's wife has on black and not white. She should know better than that!" Those looks led to the First Lady, God bless her, trying to "help" me be a "proper" minister's wife, so she pulled me to the front row and put a "white doily" (chapel cap) on my head. Okay that was it! I wasn't going back to "his" new church again! The next Sunday I went back to "my" church and it felt like everyone was thinking, "What's she doing here?" Maybe they weren't, but that's how I felt so I went back to "his" new church reluctantly. I got away with not going too often because of work, but when my kids started getting more involved in "his" new ministry I began taking more Sundays off to support them.

Jeanne D. Wilson, Ed.D.

I guess the new congregation gave up on "changing" us, or maybe we silently came to a compromise. Now, I wear "some" white on first Sunday, and I sit on the first row. I shake members' hands in the line after church, and I recently joined! Now the senior pastor is retiring and they want my husband to become the "new" pastor of this congregation.

A FEW OF THE MANY QUESTIONS I HAVE AS A NEW PASTOR'S WIFE

1. Even though I know we shouldn't, most people hold their pastor at a different level of accountability? How do I respect my husband as my pastor when I know everything about him the good, the bad, and the very ugly?

2. I wasn't called to preach, minister, or counsel but I have to believe that God has kept me with my husband this long for a reason. In the role of a pastor's wife I will end up doing all of the above, plus more. What if that's not something I want to do?

3. Is it normal to feel jealous of the church? When he was with other women, I could compare or compete! I can't compare or compete against God and the church! Sunday service, Tuesday Bible study, Wednesday prayer, Thursday school and people always needing prayer. What about me and our family?

4. Is it normal for you to feel like some of the ladies are trying to "holla" at your husband when they are asking for "prayer"? Some are because I know I'm not crazy,

My Sister's Keeper

but how should I handle it? Should I just leave it to him to handle?
Someone please help me!!!!

Jeanne D. Wilson, Ed.D.

My Sister's Keeper

I will praise thee; for I am fearfully and wonderfully made: marvelous are thy works; and that my soul knoweth right well.
Psalm 139:14

Chapter Three:
Who Am I?

LADY FLORENCE JONES

In the infamous words of the great song writer Diana Ross, she asked the world this question; "Do you know where you're going to, do you like the things that life is showing you, where are you going to, do you know?"

First of all, who are you? Do you have your own identity outside of your spouse? You may feel like a stranger to yourself, because so much of who you are is wrapped up in your husband and the ministry. Well let me share with you what was once shared with me by a very wise woman in the form of my grand-mother...Thelma C. Washington whom I fondly called "Mother".

She was the wife of a Pastor Rev. C.W. Washington, a dynamic and prolific speaker in his own right and she was involved in several facets of ministry within the church and abroad. When my husband accepted his call into the ministry, he was only 19 years old. When he (we) stepped out into the deep to Pastor a congregation, he was 25 years old. I was excited for him because I knew this was something he would do with his whole heart. When sharing with my family this exciting news, Mother and I sat down and she began sharing with me in detail her experiences. Some of them I had heard growing up; others shocked me beyond belief as to how people could sometimes be so cruel to the Pastor and his family. The time she and I spent together in hours of conversation was priceless. But there was one thing in particular that she imparted to me and I have embraced it and walked in it throughout my ministry. Her words will forever ring true for me because they are a part of the plan from God for my life. Mother told me to always be myself. Never allow others to keep me in their mental box. When God created me, He was also positioning me, molding me, and equipping me. The great calling on my life came directly from my creator and not man. She told me to not try to be a people pleaser because people get confused and don't know what they want. They will have to give an account to God for their own actions and I mine.

This was great advice to me, because I know how to do "me" real well. I was never one to conform to what others were doing anyway but I know for some of you that might be a struggle. Mother has gone on to glory and is now resting in the presence of the Heavenly Father, but her wisdom still rings true in my heart and will continue as long as I live.

To all my sisters who are married or will soon be married to Pastors, please understand who you are is made up from within.

If you are battling with fear, insecurity, depression, intimidation, or anything that keeps you hindered from walking in your God given calling, I would like to introduce you to a man named Jeremiah. When God called Jeremiah, He had to remind him of his purpose: "Jeremiah, you have to understand, before I formed you in your mothers belly, I knew you, (intimacy) I consecrated you, (cleansed) I set you apart, (holy) I appointed, (anointed) I ordained, (called) you to be the spokesperson right now in the Kingdom" (see Jeremiah. 1:5)

Jeanne D. Wilson, Ed.D.

I know from reading (Jeremiah 1:6-8) he was scared to death. He said. "Lord, I can't. I know you might have put me in my mother's belly, but I can't speak. I can't!

Please my sister realize that God has heard every excuse in the book: I can't sing, I can't play the piano, I'm not a people person, I'm an introvert, not an extrovert, I can't write, I can't teach...I, I, I! You might feel thrown into ministry, but understand, God called you before He placed you in your mother's womb and He will meet every need you have in ministry. You are already equipped for every good work. (2 Timothy 3:17)

God will ignite your role as a Pastors wife with His purpose. When we look back at Jeremiah, we see that he cried a lot. This is why he was called the "Weeping Prophet" Lord have mercy, by the time you read Jeremiah 9, this brother is totally depressed! You may be in this very same place right now, but all the Lord is asking from you is a firm yes!

Say Yes!

For those of you who are still trying to "bail", stop it...it's not going to work! You can't run nor hide from your God given purpose. If you do this, it may propel you into a depression because of disobedience. Perhaps you feel you are too young or too old, don't know anything about Christianity (a new convert) or have a hard time remembering scriptures. First Corinthians 1:27 says, "But God chose the foolish things of the world to shame the wise." God does not always call the qualified, he qualifies those HE calls.

You share the calling with your husband just like Sarai did with Abram. In Genesis.17 God finally speaks of Sarai: "As for Sarai your wife, you are no longer to call her Sarai; her name will be Sarah. I will bless hear and will surely give you a son by her. I will bless her so that she will be mother of nations; kings of people will come from her" (vv.15-16). When her name changed, her elevation did also to an exalted position beside (not behind) her husband, Abraham. She went from Sarai (leader) to Sarah which means "princess". The call of God that is on your husband is also on you. When you married him you became one with him, so the mantle that rests upon him is now resting upon you. The enabling that's in him is also in you. The authority (anointing) that resides in him resides in you. You my sister, share in all aspects of his life in ministry.

I have personally experienced the awesome blessing of this shared calling alongside my husband. He is the gifted speaker-I am not. My gifting came through music, exhortation, (encouragement) and service. No I don't play the piano, but I can sing, direct the choir, teach songs and beat the "stew" out of a tambourine (as my grand-mother would say) I love people and I don't mind extending myself to someone in need of my assistance. Through revelation, however, I realized that I could tap into my husbands' anointing and his enabling, so I speak when the opportunity arises.

I relinquished my will years ago to follow the will of God the Father for my life. He has elevated me to the place where I belong-a place alongside my husband as a Sarah, a princess, not a Queen.

Please don't refuse to embrace God's call on your life. Sarah had a momentary faith breakdown which caused her to weaken and become hopeless. She failed to realize that the mantel also rested upon her. She didn't think she could be the

Jeanne D. Wilson, Ed.D.

person needed to fulfill the call, so instead of pressing in faith, she found a "solution" to her feeling of inadequacy (see Genesis. 16:1-2). If you fail to live by faith and your lack of trusting God, you can bring dissension and confusion into your home.

Today my prayer for you is that you will position yourself in His secret place. Jeremiah 1:8 tells us "Be not afraid of them (their faces)" (AMP). Focus my sister on the face of the Lord. I pray that God would give you revelation of who you are and that he would elevate you to your rightful place alongside your husband so that you can effectively share in the calling the Lord has upon your lives. The heavenly Father of your life, and of His Church, has direction for your life. There are no cowardly soldiers serving in the army of the Lord. All He wants from you is your mind, body, soul, and spirit along with a firm yes!

Reflections

What is your purpose?

_____

_____

_____

What fear(s) have you been battling as the pastors wife?

_____

_____

_____

Plan of Action

_____

_____

_____

Jeanne D. Wilson, Ed.D.

Love is patient, love is kind. It does not envy, it does not boast, it is not proud. It is not rude, it is not self-seeking, it is not easily angered, it keeps no record of wrongs. Love does not delight in evil but rejoices with the truth. It always protects, always trusts, always hopes, always perseveres.
1 Corinthians 13:4-7

Jeanne D. Wilson, Ed.D.

Chapter Four: Remember Why He Married You

LADY STEPHANIE NORTHINGTON

Dear Sister,

So, you are now married to a preacher. Out of all of the traits that you will need, the one trait that I pray you will be blessed with is a GOOD MEMORY.

As a preacher's wife you must be comfortable being the center of attention. For me this continues to be the most difficult thing that I deal with because I am a different race than my husband. I feel as though I am the "center of attention" a lot more often than I would like to be. There have been times when we have visited churches and the pastor's wife would ask that all of the preacher's wives stand up. Being not just the only preacher's wife of another race, but being the ONLY person of another race in the room I can just see everyone's eyes going back and forth between the preachers and me trying to figure out which one I'm married to. But, even if you are the same race as your husband, you will always be the center of attention. Other women in the church will talk about you and will scrutinize your every move. You will be able to see the questions on their faces. "Why did he marry her?" "Has she gained weight?" "What is she wearing?" "Does she think she is the pastor?" "Can't she control her kids?"

There will be many times when you get up early and come to church tired or with a headache and very few other people will be there. Maybe they aren't there because it was raining or because the big game was on that day. These are the times when your husband needs you most. If no one else is there to say AMEN when he preaches, you will be there. And your marriage will be strong because of it.

There will come a time when your husband has doubts. He will need your strength and your faith to help him through. You must always be the voice of reason for him. Don't let him give up out of frustration. You can pray with him when he is unsure that God is leading him to make the right decision. You know him in many ways better than he knows himself.

All of these times are when your GOOD MEMORY is going to come in handy. When you doubt yourself and when you hear "Why did he marry her," you will need to remember the answer. He chose you out of every other woman he could have because he LOVES you. He knows that when no one else is there you will be there. He can depend on you for your unconditional love and support. Remember he needs you and you don't need the approval of every parishioner you come across. Once they get to know you they will love you too. Your husband knows your heart, sees your faith and soon the congregation will see it too.

Jeanne D. Wilson, Ed.D.

Reflections

Take a walk down memory lane. Why did you marry your husband?

_____

_____

_____

What are some qualities he loves most in you?

_____

_____

_____

What do you love most about him?

_____

_____

_____

Plan of Action

_____

_____

_____

My Sister's Keeper

And He arose, and rebuked the wind, and said unto the sea, Peace, be still. And the wind ceased, and there as a great calm.
Mark 4:39

Chapter Five:
Sit Down & Shut Up! Allowing Your Husband To Pastor Without All Your Opinions

LADY ANDREA CLARK

Get you some business!!! Every 1st Lady needs to have her own personal calendar which consists of things she needs to do outside of the church, so that she doesn't become so entangled in the affairs of the church that she forgets who the Pastor is.

If your anything like me, you have an opinion about everything; How many songs need to be sung, how the armor bearer should be able to read the pastors mind, the ushers need to exercise hand signals, and the deacons need to move quicker. I think you get my point. I am full of bright ideas and have a solution for everything. Boy, I must of lost 10 lbs when God said "Sit down and shut up!" I was like, this can't be God. But it was and He had had enough of me and what I thought.

During my time of silence, it allowed me to see that when my pastor/husband was discussing church matters or ministry ideas with me that he wasn't seeking my opinion or approval. He got enough of that from the board members. He was merrily just sharing his thoughts with me. And me with my foolish self, I would jump in mid sentence and say what I thought, or why something wasn't going to work. Thank God my comments never deterred him from what he had planned to do. But think of how much more he would of been encouraged if he knew that I really had his back. And not just faking a smile because that's what I'm supposed to do. Boy when God got my attention, He really got it. He made it clear to me that He had already given the vision for His church to the Pastor. And that the Pastor had did an excellent job in conveying it to the members. And it was the member's job to put legs to the vision. And that I was one of the members. Ouch!! Why does that still hurt today? I believe it's because I was so far off track, that I'm still embarrassed.

What it took me sometime to realize was that even when we were at home, he was still my pastor. Now hold on cause I know what you're thinking. He's the Pastor at church and a husband at home. Well sorry ladies, I go against popular opinion. I believe he's the Pastor in both places and that we should govern ourselves accordingly. See when you begin to choose what building you're going to submit to him in you run into problems. But if you stay in the mode of submission it makes it easier for you to stand alongside of him and support him as a Pastor, Husband and Father. Not always second guessing the mandate that God has given him to carry out for the church, and the responsibility that he has to lead his family. See managing up may work on the job, but it has no place in the church. (Managing up is when you consistently tell your boss what should be done, and they do it).

Ok ladies, I was trying to bring this to an end but God is making me share this story with you. One day as my husband and I were riding in the car, I was running off with the mouth as usual telling him what I liked and didn't like and what we should be doing different at the church. This must of gone on for about 30 minutes this particular day. Then all of a sudden God dropped a rhema word in my spirit "SHUT UP"! So I shared with my husband what happened and added that from this day forward, I was going to slow my roll. He hollered out, 'Thank God! I have been praying about your mouth!" I swear my face froze. I silently said a prayer that I was going to be the best member that Living Word had. I would arrive on time, give my tithes and offering and assist my Pastor only in the areas where he requested my help until I had full control of the need to talk too much.

As I look back now I think of how I could of saved myself a lot of stress and headaches and kept my little cute shape (remember I lost 10lbs when God put me in my place) if I had only lived by Hebrews 13:17. Obey your spiritual leaders and do what they say. Their work is to watch over your souls and they know they are accountable to God. Give them reason to do this joyfully and not with sorrow.

Reflections

What are some areas in ministry or your marriage where you know you need to sit down and shut up?

_____

_____

_____

What changes can you make to become a valued listener instead of a problem solver?

_____

_____

_____

Plan of Action

_____

_____

_____

Jeanne D. Wilson, Ed.D.

Let every man be swift to hear, slow to speak, slow to wrath
James 1:19

Chapter Six:
Don't Let Satan Use You!
How Information You Tell Your Husband Can Be Detrimental to His Ministry

DR. JEANNE WILSON

There will be many times in your marriage to a pastor that you will need to embody the proverbial principle of the three wise monkeys "see no evil, hear no evil, speak no evil".

In the early years of the ministry, I would tell my husband everything I knew or heard about the members, including how they felt and what they said about him.

Bro. Can't Get Right said, "The men's ministry isn't doing enough for the community."

Sis. Big mouth said, "Everybody is upset about that statement you made in church last week."

Now why in the world would he need to know all of that??

When your husband is contemplating and agonizing over the vision and direction for the church, and the congregation is whispering about the changes he wants to implement (Some members purposely say things around you so you can take that bone back to the pastor) your husband needs to know that you are his biggest fan, cheering him on like you are at a Michael Jackson concert, screaming, crying and fainting every time he gets up to preach. OK I'm taking it to the extreme but you get my point.

In hindsight, I realize that I was allowing Satan to use me to tear down my husband's spirit. Now I love that man with all my heart so I would never do anything to hurt him intentionally, yet in my feeble attempt to inform him of the murmurings of the congregation, I was adding additional unnecessary burdens to his already stressful life.

As wives we can be our husbands' support as well as their sandpaper. This is a delicate combination. Proverbs 15:1 says, "A soft answer turneth away wrath: but grievous words stir up anger." Like sandpaper we can sometimes be a little rough on them.

As wives we can also be the pastors' hardest critics. "You know if your sermon were just a little shorter it would have been much better." But it's only because we want to help smooth their rough edges so the rest of the world can see the beauty beneath that we already know exists. In your private prayer time ask the Lord to grant you wisdom and to bridle your tongue. ((James 1:26)

In our sanding we have to be careful not to rub so hard that we strip away all of their manhood.

Jeanne D. Wilson, Ed.D.

Reflections

Can you think of a time when you shared something with your husband that a member said and later realized you should not have?

_____

_____

_____

What steps will you take before sharing information that may help or hinder your husband's focus on ministry?

_____

_____

_____

Plan of Action

_____

_____

_____

My Sister's Keeper

The LORD God said, "It is not good for the man to be alone. I will make a helper suitable for him."
Genesis 2:18

Jeanne D. Wilson, Ed.D.

Chapter Seven:
Do I Have to Go to Go to Church Again? Preventing Burn Out in Ministry

Lady Rebecca Miller

I have been a pastor's wife for just as long as I have been married which is seventeen years. My husband acknowledged his "call" to ministry just before we got married, and I had no idea what I was getting into. I never really grew up in the church so I was ignorant of what was expected of me by others and God. I took the title of minister's wife as being able to say, "Yeah I caught a good man! He is good looking AND a preacher!!" I did not realize that could be a blessing and a curse at the same time.

As God started opening doors for him I found myself going to every fellowship he was going to. We would be in church four sometimes five nights a week plus two to three services on Sundays depending on where he was invited to preach. I was worn out for years but didn't have a true understanding of what was expected of me. I was burned out so, why in the world did I find myself going to EVERYTHING??!!

The reason why I found myself going to nearly every fellowship, appreciation or church function of any sort is because I have to be my husband's cheerleader. He needs to know I support him and nobody has got his back like I do.

It took me some time to finally realize my husband does not need me to be at every function to know how much I support him. As he was called to the ministry, I was called to minister to him. He needs to know I am in his corner and will stick with him in any decision he makes, whether I think it good or bad.

When he was tired I was to comfort him, when he was angry I was to be the voice of reason and when he didn't know what to say I was to sit in silence along with him. I have seen disappointment, excitement, anger, hurt and surprise sometimes all in the same day.

Get ready because if you ride to service together you may be the first one to arrive and the last one to leave the building. Sometimes after a revival or a service my husband needs to minister to members or he might want to hang out with his friends. Now we drive two separate cars to service so he does not have to worry about me telling him I am ready to go.

We now have an understanding that the reason I'm always ready to go is to get back to my other duties as a mother, which include caring for the house and being available for our children. Family is very important to us and we have developed our relationship enough to where we both understand that there needs to be a clear balance of church and home. My husband understands that I need to provide that balance because that is my strong point and I understand he needs to fellowship and bond with his brothers in the ministry. God has given each of us our place in our relationship to work together and continue to grow closer to Him as a couple and as a family.

In our journey together my husband has shown me what true and real love for Christ is. I have grown so much

Jeanne D. Wilson, Ed.D.

under his pastoral leadership that I am in total awe of Christ every day. Praise the Lord!!

Reflections

How do you balance being a wife, raising children, working, and meeting church responsibilities?

_____

_____

_____

Are you feeling over whelmed and stressed? What steps will you take to set boundaries and convey your need for balance to your family, friends and congregation?

_____

_____

_____

Plan of Action

_____

_____

_____

Jeanne D. Wilson, Ed.D.

My Sister's Keeper

Strength and dignity are her clothing and her position is strong and secure...
Proverbs 31:25

Chapter Eight:
How 70's T.V. Shows Can Help You Be a Better Pastor's Wife

LADY GENEA S. BRICE

At first glance, I know this title seems a bit odd. But, you must admit, however, it is intriguing. It makes you want to find out just what I mean, doesn't it? Well, hopefully after perusing the next few paragraphs, you will be both enlightened and encouraged by the nuggets of truth and life lessons revealed. Read on, my sister!

Life Lesson#1: "The Incredible Hulk."

My first few years at our new church found me all at once both anxious and curious. I so wanted to "get busy" meeting and greeting all of the new people I saw and find out "what was what". Getting involved with ministries and being a part of something greater than myself appealed to me immensely. Parenthetically, I am a rather exuberant person by nature I love people and I embrace life with both hands, fully intending to live it to the fullest (even as I write this, I am smiling ear to ear). I also tend to believe the best in people. I was in store for some rather abrupt reality checks per our new assignment.

One day a particular ministry was putting on a program and I was asked to lend a helping hand. The day came and I was ready. At the time, my daughter was only two years old, so I brought her along with me. The person in charge came to me and said, "Sis. Brice, we are going to need your help. You can put your daughter in the office with a video and a pizza." Now, as you can imagine, my heart was pounding, my pulse was racing and I could feel heat rising from somewhere near my toes, up to my neck and resting on top of my head. I wanted to say in the immortal words of Dr. Bruce Banner, "Don't make me angry. You wouldn't like me when I'm angry."

Now, here's the lesson I learned that day: No matter how nice, calm, cool and collected we think we are; no matter how put together and subdued we are as The First Lady, we all possess the potential to act in some very un-Christian-like ways. I hate to admit it, but I was really about to go smooth off and tell that lady where to go and how to get there. I mean, how dare she presume to tell me what to do with my daughter and on top of that make such an asinine suggestion as to put a two year-old in an office alone! The nerve! I was angry. No, let me re-phrase: I WAS HOT! And at that moment, I needed something greater than me to control me. I needed something greater than me to control my thoughts, my hands and my tongue. Without the indwelling of the Holy Spirit in the life of the believer, we simply cannot live a life pleasing to the Lord, no, not even the First Lady. I learned that day that there truly is "a war in my members" and when I would do good, evil is present with me. It is the power of the Holy Ghost that makes living for the Lord possible. The Holy Spirit is a restrainer and a constrainer who allows us to overcome without unleashing the monster within.

For further study and edification, please read(Romans 7:14-25; and Job 32:18)

Jeanne D. Wilson, Ed.D.

Life Lesson #2: "The Six Million Dollar Man."

I can remember sitting in our living room as a child, glued to the T.V. set watching *The Six Million Dollar Man*. It was one of my all-time favorites. I can remember the scene where his rocket ship collided with the ground and he lay there clinging to life. Then that voice came on saying, "Steve Austin. A man barely alive. We can re-build him....." spoken by that faithful helper, Oscar Goldman. I was hooked. Every week, you could find me at the same time, in the same place.

This scene came rushing back to me as I recalled an incident in my life not long ago. It was one of those Sundays when I was finding it hard to praise. The morning was hard, the children were moving slow, my husband was complaining, and, of course, we were running late-again. By the time I got to church, I was, quite frankly, spent. I must admit, I didn't hear one note the choir sang that day; I can't tell you what the sermon was about, and if the deacons prayed, I hope they prayed for me. I had had it that day. Out of utter desperation and exasperation, I cried out unto the Lord from somewhere deep within. It was then that the Spirit of the Lord came quietly and spoke deep into my soul. He said, "I know you don't feel like it, but you are valuable—most valuable to me. I have entrusted great treasure in earthen vessels. I have entrusted you with my word. I could have used anything to share my word concerning my son, but I have chosen you. You are most valuable to me. Remember that, my child." It was then that the words of Oscar Goldman came rushing back to me by way of the Holy Ghost: "We can re-build her. She can be better than she was before. Better. Stronger. Faster."

Steve Austin was given a new eye, new legs, and a new arm that cost a fortune. By the aid of the Holy Spirit, I got a new perspective, a new song, and a new praise. And it cost Jesus his life. I could see better, run faster, and leap higher, all because of the treasure God had invested in me. Hallelujah!

For further study and edification please read II Corinthians 4:7.

Life Lesson #3: "Wonder Woman".

The life of the First Lady is not an easy one. There are joys along the way, to be sure. But, by and large, she must be present, she must be patient, and she must be polished at all times. It gets exhausting. The needs of the congregation seem ubiquitous as her husband is needed for this event or that emergency. She, herself, may be called on to minister to a specific need, not to mention trying to rear "the pastor's kids". Let's face it: expectations are high, the needs are many and sometimes you just don't feel it. You have to smile when you feel like crying. Have to push a praise when you'd much rather not. Though my experiences are unique to me, I can share some universal truths I learned by watching another favorite 70's T.V. show: *Wonder Woman!* There are two very specific examples I have gleaned from the life of Diana Prince aka Wonder Woman:

1) "The Invisible Jet".

You must possess something invisible to the naked eye, but it keeps you flying high!! Wonder Woman had an invisible jet that transported her swiftly from one place to another. She knew it was there, but no one else could see it. So it is in the life of the First Lady: you must possess that special something that keeps you afloat amid the sometimes treacherous waters of life. You must be able to call upon something that will lift you out of whatever slump, funk or mess you are in . Others won't know it; others won't be able to see it, and they certainly won't understand it. They won't understand why you praise God anyway. Even when all hell is breaking loose and nothing is going as planned, the First Lady relies on that one peculiar, indispensable, invisible Helper called the Holy Spirit she can fly! She can be instantly transported out of gloom, doom, frustration and yes, even depression, because God always makes a way of escape!

2) "It's All in the Accessories!"

Now, personal upkeep runs a close second behind spiritual upkeep, in my book. Historically, one of the unspoken job descriptions outlined for the First Lady is that of "Fashion Mogul". Traditionally, it was the First Lady who set the fashion tone for the congregation (whether by overt action or accidental choice that morning). What she wears speaks volumes about who she is. I didn't create the rule, but I do know it definitely exists.

Remember Wonder Woman's outfit? She wore that patriotic red, white, and blue sort-of-swimsuit-get-up that was set off by those nifty knee boots with the gold stripe up the middle. And what set off that gold stripe? Those gold bracelets! They deflected bullets and brought the whole ensemble together. Talk about multi-tasking!! You remember, don't you?! Now, I am not suggesting that First Lady walk into her church on Sunday morning with a patriotic swim suit on. That would be funny, wouldn't it?! Can you imagine the stares? But what

My Sister's Keeper

I am suggesting is that we take a page from Wonder Woman, on this wise: Her name is Wonder Woman. She was able to hold down a good government job, soar head and shoulders above the rest, keep those she cared for safe from harm, all while being spit shined and polished with perfect hair, no less! Sounds like a First lady to me. Keep yourselves up, ladies. Keep your hair and nail appointments. Get massages, go on vacations. Life is too short to look bad.

We must keep in mind, then, that the true beauty of the First Lady does not come from what she wears on the outside, it is what she wears on the inside. She must put on the whole armor of God, so that she may be able to stand in the evil day.

For further study and edification please read Proverbs 31 and Ephesians 6.

In conclusion, I pray that what I have shared has been helpful. It is my prayer that what proceeds out of my mouth is both edifying and encouraging to those who hear it; or in this case, those who read it. God speaks. He will use some surprising means to get a message across. Who knew you could learn so much about the word of God from watching 70's T.V. shows? And who knew that it could help one in this ministry called "The First Lady"?

As you continue to walk, I pray that you tame the monster within, remember that you have been entrusted with a great treasure on the inside, keep relying on that invisible thing to transport you oh, and one more................to boldly go where no First Lady has gone before!! Be blessed!

Jeanne D. Wilson, Ed.D.

Reflections

What is your invisible jet? What keeps you flying high?

_____

_____

_____

What scripture will you repeat to give you peace in the midst of your storm?

_____

_____

_____

Plan of Action

_____

_____

_____

My Sister's Keeper

Better is open rebuke than love that is hidden. Faithful are the wounds of a friend; but the kisses of an enemy are deceitful
Proverbs 27:5-6

Chapter Nine: The Church as the Other Women... & Games Women Play: Keeping it Real with Old School Knowledge

Lady. Mattie W. Abner

Like most women, I never wanted to be married to a preacher for a lot of reasons. Seeing various sides of how they were treated by their husband and members made me never want to be a pastor's wife, but the Lord said something different. When my husband received his "call" I was torn asunder big time. This would be a day that would change our lives forever.

Sunday morning our choir sang, "God Willed It So" and my husband said he had heard me sing it before but never like I did in that particular service. This struck me as odd because he never responded to my singing. After we got home our world turned upside down. It was then that I figured out what was happening within him. I called my daddy and explained the state of mind his son-in-law was in. Daddy told me to go to him and say, "Speak Lord, Thy Servant Heareth", and then put him on the phone. I left him to talk to my daddy alone. So many things changed in the course of that day.

After 40+ years of marriage and 30+ years serving in ministry, I have observed many interesting things in ministry. The Pastor should set the tone in his assigned congregation. Many pastors talk about prioritizing and balancing life when they aren't doing a good job of it themselves. A wife sometimes only knows what her husband's voice sounds like when he is teaching or preaching because at home he's usually working on a sermon, praying, or counseling others. Everything and everyone can come before his wife and family, and he may be totally blind to his wife who suffers in silence.

There's a song that says, "Lord I Want To Live For Thee Everyday and Hour, Let Thy Spirit Be With Me In It's Saving Power." Let that song get in your spirit and it will keep you when women go openly after your husband. To the young pastors wife who wrote the first letter asking, "Is it normal for you to feel like some ladies are trying to "holla" at your husband?" You are NOT crazy and YES every now and then some of them are. So listen as I impart some of what you young folks call "old school" wisdom.

1. Often women will wear very, very low cut blouses, and short skirts up to their panty line.... Politely show them how to use a safety pin and hand them a lap scarf.

2. Some women want to be in the pastors' face and personal space more than they should be. Explain that there is a proper way to hug your pastor which does not include a double armed choke hold hanging around his neck like a piece of jewelry while peering up into his eyes.

3. The Pastor should not have a female member driving him around, either his wife, his children, or a male member should be his driver. Better than that, he can drive himself around or hop on a bus to get to where he has to go.

4. The pastor should not accept gifts that are too personal like t-shirts and underwear. It's the Pastor's place to make this known in whatever setting this needs to be addressed.

5. A wise pastor will not counsel women in a closed setting without the presence of another person. He should not pay late night or early morning "prayer request" visits to the homes of any women without his wife.

6. Some women come to church to see what the First Lady is wearing. They want to know why she wears hats or why she doesn't. They want to know where she buys her suits, her stockings, shoes, etc...trying to figure out how much she paid for her outfit. They are watching you for all the wrong reasons. You don't have to be a fashion model. Dress to impress yourself not others.

7. Some women argue about what the pastor likes and dislikes right in front of you as if he's their man instead of their Pastor. Politely remind them with a smile that no one knows what he prefers better than you and if ever a suggestion is needed all they need to do is ask.

8. A Pastor should sometimes have his wife stand beside him at the door or in front of the pulpit for benediction. Why? Some members go out of their way to run over visitors to get to the pastor, but pass his wife right by saying, "Oh I didn't see you." Yeah right!

My Sister's Keeper

9. The vindictive woman will pick-up on the pastors lack of regard for his family and the wife's insecurities very quickly, especially if they hear she thinks of the church as the other woman and is jealous of the time the pastor has to spend away from their family. This makes it easy for her to run over or disrespect the wife or God forbid try to make her move on her husband. Like that old commercial said, "Never let them see you sweat." Don't wear your emotions on your sleeve so your insecurities can not be so easily detected.

But it's not about being jealous of the church, it goes far beyond that. It's about the situations that continue to arise that are not addressed. Sometimes you might want to set up an appointment with your Pastor. Yes he is your husband, but it's your Pastor that you want to meet with. Unless he's pigheaded he has to hear you as a member of his congregation, not his wife. You can meet him in his office or at a restaurant and then raise all your hurts, angers, concerns, etc.

As the pastors wife you will need to stay prayed up at all times. Remember Proverbs 3:5-6. It should be your daily scripture without a doubt. There will be many nights and days you are left alone and you may get angry, feel left out, and wonder where you fit into the scheme of things. Just know that Jesus will step in just when you need him the most.

Jeanne D. Wilson, Ed.D.

Reflections

Do you need to "set an appointment" to talk about any situations or topics with your "pastor?" (Not your husband but your pastor)

_____

_____

_____

Do you have clear boundaries set up with your husband when it comes to interacting with women in the church?

_____

_____

_____

Plan of Action

_____

_____

_____

My Sister's Keeper

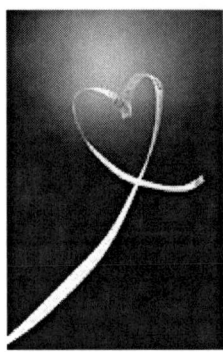

And when you fast, do not look gloomy like the hypocrites, for they disfigure their faces that their fasting may be seen by others. Truly, I say to you, they have received their reward. But when you fast, anoint your head and wash your face, [18]that your fasting may not be seen by others but by your Father who is in secret. And your Father who sees in secret will reward you.

Matthew 6:16-18

Chapter Ten:
First Ladies & Fasting

LADY CINDY EPPS

My words of wisdom to another minister's wife would be to develop a regular prayer and devotion time with God. It doesn't matter what time of day as long as it is <u>***devoted***</u> to God. You should also develop a time of regular fasting. I like to live by the words, "*Praying* is telling God what you want, *Fasting* is telling God how bad you want it." From my personal experience, I can say that God has worked miracles in and through my life because of my prayer and fasting time with Him.

Often, people will tell you that you can come to them when and if you need help, but when you really need them, they are not available. God had to become my best friend and my confidant. Because of this I have seen Him work things out for my good and speak to my husband about things that were going on with me that I couldn't speak of myself. God has also told me things about my husband, and my husband didn't have to say a word. I truly believe God's favor has been upon my marriage and my life because of my prayer life. I dare you to give Prayer and Fasting a try!

Reflections

Write a list of needs that you are asking God for in your life.

1. _____

2. _____

3. _____

4. _____

5. _____

Plan of Action

Purchase a book on fasting. Find one that meets your spiritual and physical needs (Consult your doctor before you begin if you have health issues)

Books for your reference: *Fasting for a Spiritual Breakthrough* or *The Beginner's Guide to Fasting*

Jeanne D. Wilson, Ed.D.

Look carefully then how you walk, not as unwise but as wise, making the best use of the time, because the days are evil.

Ephesians 5:15-16

Chapter Eleven:
Super Saint, Wonder Wife, Bible Believing Barbie – Balancing Ministry without Losing Yourself

DR. JEANNE WILSON

As a pastor's wife it is very easy to lose focus of who you are. While under the members microscope, you will be talked about for things you do well and scrutinized and ostracized for things you do not. I have often asked myself: Who am I? How can I please God in this role? How will I balance working a full time job; raise happy, well rounded children; maintain the household bills and chores; be a good wife to my husband at home, while supporting him in ministry, which also means assisting him in supporting the needs of the congregation.

One day a good friend who is a pastor asked, "How do you and Wilson work so well together in ministry? My wife and I have tried but we end up arguing because all she wants to do is talk about church."

Boy do I remember those days. At the dinner table, "Dwayne what do think about a power point projector and screen so the words to songs and your sermons can be displayed?" In the car, "Honey what about purchasing a church van so we can pick people up from the local community?" And yes, even in the bed watching television, "A lot of the couples in the church are hurting in their relationships. What do you

Jeanne D. Wilson, Ed.D.

think about us doing monthly relationship seminars? We can call it Couples4Christ. What do you think?" One day during one of my marvelous ideas (and believe me I had lots of them) Dwayne stopped me mid-sentence and said, "Can we not talk about church stuff at home. Home is my sanctuary where I come and know I can find peace. I need you to be my wife when we are at home. I just want to relax and laugh and hang out with you and the kids not talk about ministry." It reminds me of the story of Isaac and Rebecca (Genesis 24). Rebecca is introduced as a brave, beautiful and resourceful young woman who loves and respects her husband. She cooked, she cleaned, she impressed everyone who met her. She seemed like the perfect match for Isaac. After she gave birth to twin boys, Esau and Jacob, Rebecca changed. As was tradition the oldest twin (Esau) was to act as the head of the household if his father died. Rebecca wanted her favorite son, the youngest twin, to lead instead so she manipulated the situation, and tricked her poor, blind, old, dying husband into believing that the youngest twin he was giving his blessing to was really the oldest. I can imagine before she went to such extremes she, like me had many conversations to try and persuade Isaac in her direction. "Isaac, you know Jacob would be a better head of the household. Isaac, what do you think about Jacob doing a trial "head of the household" test run before you head on to glory, you'll see, he'll be great!"

How did this loyal helpmate go from being a humble, loving wife to being a know it all, busybody? **Proverbs 12:4 says,** "A virtuous woman is a crown to her husband: but she that doth things worthy of confusion is a rottenness in his bones." Unknowingly I was becoming like Rebecca to my husband. In wanting the best *for him*, I had become an irritant *to him*.

That was the beginning of us setting boundaries and my learning to separate my husband from my pastor. In setting these new boundaries I was released from the invisible burdens that I had placed on myself. I did not have to be Super Saint, Wonder Wife, or Bible Believing Barbie, all I had to be was Jeanne.

That's when I decided to continue my education and return to school to obtain my doctorate degree. I "got myself some business" as Lady Andrea Clark said.

Returning to school allowed me to take my focus off my husbands' ministry and place it on me. Now that may sound selfish to some but what those four years of school did was allow us time to define our clear cut roles in ministry. He is the pastor and I am his wife, his helpmate in all things that matter greatly to him. I messed up before because I was trying to be his helpmate in all things "I thought" should matter greatly to him. There was a major difference between the two.

Reflections

How are you guilty in speaking about the ministry 24/7?

_____

_____

_____

What do you do outside of church to enhance your personal life? What would you like to do?

_____

_____

_____

Plan of Action

_____

_____

_____

My Sister's Keeper

"Shouldn't you have had mercy on your fellow servant just as I had on you?' In anger his master turned him over to the jailers to be tortured, until he should pay back all he owed. This is how my heavenly Father will treat each of you unless you forgive your brother from your heart."
Matthew 18:33-35

Jeanne D. Wilson, Ed.D.

Chapter Twelve:
Is She Really After Man?

ANONYMOUS

My testimony began over 25 years ago when a young woman entered our ministry and also became a part of our office staff. At first I overlooked the times that she would find herself in my husband's presence; after all she was on the staff and it only seemed natural that she would always be around.

One Sunday; however, a seasoned saint warned me that while she was in prayer the Lord let her know that this woman was sent to this city and to our church to destroy my husband's ministry. Just getting started in ministry and loving the Lord my husband was oblivious to the entire thing, nonetheless, she didn't hesitate even though he had not acknowledged her advances.

There was one incident that occurred when I knew I had to approach her. My husband needed emergency surgery and no one except my husband and I along with his ministerial confidant knew of this as well as what hospital he was in. Therefore, I was more than surprised for her to make it to the hospital before I did (flowers in hand). His confident had made her aware of the situation and she appeared. Needless to say, I questioned the confidant as to his part in this situation. I subsequently spoke to her regarding her actions and her only response was: "I knew he was married, but I didn't know you were his wife", (Yes, she made this statement even though she had been trying to befriend me during this time).

After realizing what she was capable of, I told her that our church was not large enough for both of us and I gently suggested that she find other employment and another place of worship. After an embarrassing altercation she agreed but she didn't leave the congregation for about a year.

I became bitter and mad at the very sight of her, and for a while I felt justified. After all, my friends told me that I was justified; my spiritual advisor told me I was justified. However being raised by Godly parents I knew in my heart that I was not justified and God was not pleased with my attitude, so I sought Him for a willingness to forgive her. It was, by far, the hardest thing that had ever plagued my life, but I wanted so much to please God so there was only one option. I began to seek the Lord for his help and at first nothing changed. Then, I was advised to pray for her three times per day and I did. While I was praying about her, God showed how far away I had gotten from Him. I was so angry and bitter I felt like if I saw her on the street, I would run her over with my car. You see I was in bad shape.

Finally, I went to the altar one Sunday night and wept. That night God did surgery on my heart I was free to forgive as I had been forgiven. I went home that evening and called her long distance and asked her to forgive me. I subsequently saw her at a church gathering a year or so later and we greeted each other and I praised God that I loved her with the love of the Lord. The bitterness and resentment were done and I knew I was free and I will tell anybody that asks, it wasn't until I became willing to allow God to forgive through me that it was accomplished.

Jeanne D. Wilson, Ed.D.

Reflections

Mark 11:25-26 says "And when you stand praying, if you hold anything against anyone, forgive them, so that your Father in heaven may forgive you your sins."

Who do you need to forgive today?

_____

_____

_____

_____

What steps will you take to begin the process?

_____

_____

_____

_____

Plan of Action

_____

_____

_____

_____

My Sister's Keeper

And we know that all things work together for good to them that love God, to them who are the called according to his purpose.
Romans 8:28

Chapter Thirteen:
I Quit-Life After Divorce

MINISTER CATHY BRYANT-NELSON

Dear Woman of God,

 I am honored to be a part of a project that will benefit so many women of God, especially Pastor's Wives (PW). When I became a P.W. there was little to no information to help guide my understanding and role as a PW.

 My husband at the time was a well advanced "crack" user. I was naive to this world of drugs that almost destroyed my family, but he had a desire to get off "crack cocaine" so I began to help him with his quest. He never entered a treatment program because after trying one it did not work for him. One day in the living room he cried out to God, "Take this disease away from me!" A few days later it was gone. I could not believe it. He was drug free. He began to seek out men of God that could help rebuild his self esteem and help him become a father to his children (six boys and two girls) and a husband to his wife once again.

 One day he told me he heard the voice of God call him to do ministry. I thought to myself, "You! You used to be a crackhead, God can't be calling you. Let me talk to HIM on your behalf because you must not have heard him correctly." He began wrestling in his sleep and sweating at odd hours of the day. I didn't know what was wrong with him. I thought he had gone back to using again. Then one day in church he went down for prayer and announced he had received his "calling" from the Lord. In my mind I said "O Lord this cannot be happening to me." At first I was very much afraid and scared.

As he began preparing to preach his first sermon, I was all nerves and shaking in my skin, no boots! After some time he was ordained and began to work as a called ambassador for Christ. Things went well for the first few years, then he was up for selection to pastor a church. I said, "Can't you be content working alongside a pastor and not have your own church." Well, that brought about a disagreement which lasted some time, but then I began to seek the Lord, because I had no idea what I was supposed to do. I had seen other minister's wives but no guidance was given to me personally.

One day, a Pastor's wife invited me to a luncheon for PW only. There, I began to feel I found a place where I could get answers to my many questions. As I became familiar with other pastors wives, I felt comforted and comfortable and gained some understanding and expectations about PWs. I met with these ladies once a month to have lessons, plan programs, luncheons, and would visit their churches for special anniversaries.

One day, one of the mothers from the church mother's board called me out for lunch and took me shopping for a new suit that would be pleasing in the eyes of the older congregation because they did not like my African attire. She dressed me from hat to toe. At first I loved it, but it took away my personal identity and I didn't like that. I began to feel resentment toward the Pastor, my husband.

Jeanne D. Wilson, Ed.D.

He was spending more time worrying about the churches needs than my own and our family needs. We began to argue every weekend leading up to Sunday morning, when we were supposed to look all holy and righteous! "I thought in my mind "FORGET THOSE PEOPLE!" But like a good wife I showed up with a smile on my face while crying in my heart, just to be by the Pastor's side. Besides the people were paying his salary and the least I could do was show my face, even if I wasn't happy.

Soon I began to resent my position and the calling church people began to place upon me. These were expectations that I did not desire to live up too. I told my husband I did not want to go to church anymore. I quit!!!!

After that conversation, every Sunday was a struggle to get dressed and put on my "church face". In my heart I began to hate these people and him too. I stopped answering calls from various members and even stopped going to the monthly pastor's wives luncheon. I stopped everything because I began to lose who I was and felt no one could help me. I hated being married and even more I hated being a pastor's wife. I began to make excuses for not attending bible study, and then found creative ways to stay home on Sunday's.

My kids were so stressed out because they were "always" expected to be on good behavior in the sight of the "righteous ones". Although I do believe the church members loved my kids, they held them to a standard that was unrealistic. My husband even held them to a holy standard that was crazy. They could not just be kids because they were representing the first family and they were never to embarrass their father at church.

We did seek marriage counseling from a trusted pastor and his wife and things began to change for the better but I still felt in my heart that my husband was not covering me as his wife as the Bible says.

After six years our marriage ended. Being a pastors' wife was too much pressure for me. Such high and unattainable expectations were placed on me from so many. Members wanted me to have all the answers and attend all the meetings and jump when they say how high.

After our divorce it took some time; I prayed, returned to school and focused on raising my children. I also found a new church home. I was finally able to find "me" again. I am truly thankful for the mature growth I have developed in Christ Jesus over the years which helped me to forgive and find joy again. Although those were painful years, through adversity, my journey has made me a unique, set apart and whole woman in God. Isaiah 12:2 Surely God is my salvation, I will trust and not be afraid.

Jeanne D. Wilson, Ed.D.

Reflections

Is the pressure of being a Pastor's wife becoming too much for you? Name two things you would like to change.

_____

_____

_____

_____

We sometimes add undue pressure on ourselves. Have you asked your husband what *he* expects from his first lady?

_____

_____

_____

_____

Plan of Action

_____

_____

_____

_____

My Sister's Keeper

We can make our plans, but the LORD determines our steps.
Proverbs 16:9 (NLT)

Chapter Fourteen:
Break Up to Make Up –
Reconciled Marriages

Lady Denise Clark

When I received the invitation to write a letter for this book, I was a little apprehensive but I was quickly reminded that my experience wasn't just for me. If we are real with people by letting them know what we've been through, there will be a serious breakthrough in the body of Christ. So I am writing this letter to help and share with other women who may be hurting.

Philippians 4:13 is one of my favorite scriptures. I can do all things through Christ who strengthens me. That scripture brought me joy on many days, during my reconciliation with my husband. I had to grasp in my mind that God loved me so much that he would get me through my pain.

My husband and I met in church when we were really young. As we matured and started dating, what stands out most is how much fun we had together. We would laugh as we walked down the River Ben or in the French Quarters and we loved to lay by the lake and eat crawfish. When he moved to California he soon became one of the youngest pastors in the Bay Area. Not long after I relocated from New Orleans to California to get married.

After being married only two short years an act of infidelity was committed in my marriage. I had two small babies, and the only friends I had were those who were members of my husband's congregation. I thought like many women, "This cannot be happening to me," especially since he was a man of God, but it did.

The first few months were very difficult. Although I continued to go to church I didn't want to be there. I had a hard time hearing the word of God preached by him. When we first married, I was convinced that the man I married was the man God gave to me, but when I was going through my storm, I thought, "There is no way God could have given me that man!" As he was up preaching, I would sit in my seat and think, "You need to practice what you preach!" I was angry, disgruntled and did not trust anyone at church anymore.

The title of this chapter is Break Up to Make Up – Reconciled Marriages; How many of you know you can break up and still live in the same house? Just going through the motions like zombies, we were mentally broken; emotionally separated in the home by hurt, lies and deceit.

Our healing process began when we sought godly counsel from a licensed Christian marriage counselor, Dr. Craig Adams. Not only did we go to marriage counseling together but we also knew it was important to seek individual therapy as well. It was in counseling that the therapist encouraged me to confront my husband about everything. After asking the hard questions and hearing the answers that were even harder to hear, the healing began.

Therapy made me take a hard look at myself. Had I been ignoring and not meeting my husband's needs? I knew I loved him and we were compatible but I had to take more time to discover what he needed from me as his wife.

Jeanne D. Wilson, Ed.D.

As I continued to pray for God to restore my marriage, I realized I had to be willing to forgive my husband, and let God heal my heart. That was one of the hardest things in the world for me to do, since I had a problem with forgiveness. Over time, God not only restored my marriage, but he has allowed reconciliation between me and the woman and loving acceptance of their child.

If you have been hurt or betrayed by your husband any time during your marriage trust God! If you are willing to LET GO AND LET GOD he can and will restore your marriage. We can't do it in our own strength, but we can do all things through Christ!

Reflections

If you and your husband were to have a session with a marriage counselor what issues would be brought up?

_____

_____

_____

Are there any areas in your marriage that you need to "Let Go and Let God" handle?

_____

_____

_____

Plan of Action

Do you need to make an appointment for couples or individual counseling today?

_____

_____

_____

Jeanne D. Wilson, Ed.D.

Pleasant words are as an honeycomb, sweet to the soul, and health to the bones.
Proverbs 16:24

Chapter Fifteen:
Show Her Your Love-Practical Advice for Pastors & Parishioners

DR. JEANNE WILSON

To Pastors:

Man of God, make time for your wife! In ministry "quantity" time is not a reality but, "quality" time is a choice that needs to be made intentionally and deliberately. As a pastor God has given you a great responsibility, not only to the church but also to your family. I Timothy 3:5 says, "If a man does not know how to rule his own house how shall he take care of God's house." God gave you a wife to help meet your needs. If nurtured, supported and uplifted by you, she will be able to help your ministry flourish.

How the pastor treats his wife is exactly how the congregation will receive her. You are the thermometer to which the members will follow. A **thermometer** is an instrument used to measure the degree of hotness or coldness of a body or environment. How is your lack of attention to the gift God gave you altering the temperature in your environment?

Your members are watching you! They are watching your facial expressions, listening to comments you make to and about her, watching when you think no one is looking to see how you interact when no one is around. How you uplift and respect her in front of the church with verbal and non-verbal communication will determine if the church is hot or cold towards her. The congregation treats her exactly how you do, either with love, respect and admiration or they will ignore, disregard and at times disrespect her because they see that's exactly what you do!

My husband always says, "Give me my flowers while I can still smell them!" Remember how you romanced your wife in the beginning.

Compliment her hair, her outfit, her cooking. Surprise her with a getaway weekend. Clean the house, run her a bath and stick a fluffy towel in the dryer, dry her off and give her a massage or better yet, hire a maid and send her to the spa!

As Stevie Wonder says, "Show her your love...with a dozen roses." She will appreciate your appreciation.

Don't Forget the Children: I asked our two girls, Morgan (12) and Kennedy (10) what they liked and disliked about being the pastors daughters. Kennedy said, "I don't like that I don't get to spend a lot of time with my daddy. He's usually working on business work or church work. I would really like to spend some time with my very own hard working daddy." Imagine how shocked I was to hear my ten-year-old clearly communicate what she needs. She needs to feel loved by her daddy and she equates that love with just spending "a little" time with him.

I was crushed to hear how my oldest daughter Morgan felt as well. She said, "I don't like anything about it. No matter what, someone is always watching you! If I do or say one tiny thing it goes right back to my parents. Sometimes it's ok being the pastor's daughter but I really wish I could just be a regular church member."

Remember that your kids are not Stepford children. Although some "church people" (notice I did not say Christians) will expect your child to be perfect; you don't need to place those same unrealistic expectations on them.

At least once a week, take 30 minutes to sit and "listen" to your children. If you are a pastor I'm sure you have the gift of gab but your children need you to "listen" not lecture.

Plan one day a month that is just daddy & me day where you will take them for ice cream, a movie, the park, a sporting event or maybe just sit and watch a movie or their favorite show together. No cell phones, no texting, no laptops, just focused attention from daddy.

We don't want our children growing up to resent God, the church, and us as parents because we spent so much time nurturing and meeting the needs of the congregation that we forgot about the beautiful garden at home that was wilting and full of weeds, dying for love and attention. Daddy's time, acceptance, verbal expressions of approval and, most importantly, unconditional love are the water our children need to flourish.

To Parishioners:

I encourage you to love and embrace your pastors wife for she is often overlooked and ignored. (I must say I have been very blessed in this area. Thanks RCF for always showing me love.) Find out when her birthday is, find out what she likes and surprise her with a "just because" gift every now and then.

Remember to love and accept your pastor's wife for who she is and don't try to confine her to the pastor's wife box that "you think" she should be in; instead pray and ask God to mold her into the woman of faith and helpmate her husband needs and the vessel that God will be pleased with.

Don't Forget their Children

The pastors kids (PK's) can be unfairly labeled as bad, fast (girls) , spoiled etc. Don't be so quick to judge. (**Mat 7:1**) Our children are no worse than yours. They need and will appreciate your showing them love and acceptance. Kennedy also said, "I like being the pastors' daughter because I get a lot of attention and people love and care about me. I also like it because on our appreciation service, I get gifts from the children's ministry and gifts from the members of the church." The sacrifice of time spent away from her father is counterbalanced because she feels the members love her "everyday" and they show her their love and appreciation once a year. It is said it takes a village to raise a child, help your pastor raise happy, healthy, well adjusted children. Treat them as your own and don't be too quick to scrutinize and talk about them. Instead be that auntie, uncle, mentor for them to model. When you see them doing wrong you can speak the truth in love (**Eph. 4: 15**) and they will be accepting because they know you care.

If his family feels loved, accepted, and appreciated then your pastor will have a peaceful home, allowing him to study and focus on his message and ministry, instead of messy members and a miserable marriage. I guarantee these simple acts of

Jeanne D. Wilson, Ed.D.

kindness towards the pastors' family will have a trickledown effect of harmony, peace and love within the entire congregation.

Reflections for Pastors

List three things you know your wife loves that you can do for her over the next two weeks.

1. _____

   _____

2. _____

   _____

3. _____

   _____

In an effort to take time out for your children as you do for the church, ask your kids what they would like to do exclusively with you for "Daddy & Me" Day.

_____

_____

_____

Plan of Action

_____

_____

_____

Jeanne D. Wilson, Ed.D.

Reflections for Parishioners

What are some ways you will show your pastor's wife love this month?

_____

_____

_____

Do you feel the pastor's children should be held to a higher level of accountability? Why or Why not?

_____

_____

_____

Plan of Action

_____

_____

_____

My Sister's Keeper

Likewise, teach the older women to be reverent in the way they live, not to be slanderers or addicted to much wine, but to teach what is good. Then they can train the younger women to love their husbands and children, to be self-controlled and pure, to be busy at home, to be kind, and to be subject to their husbands, so that no one will malign the word of God.
Titus 2:3-5

Chapter Sixteen:
How to Start Your Own Support Group

DR. JEANNE WILSON

One day I was having lunch with a good friend whose husband had been appointed to pastor a new congregation three years prior. As lunch progressed we laughed about old times and joked about who was a bigger shopaholic. Suddenly the conversation took on a more serious tone when my friend said, "I hate that he is the pastor of a church now." As the conversation continued, I listened as she painfully described her feelings of loneliness, isolation and frustration in ministry. As I tried to encourage her, I asked if she had a mentor (another pastor's wife) that she could call on for support. Her answer astonished me. She said, "I don't know any other pastors wives except you. That's why I enjoy our annual lunches." My heart was heavy. Once a year for two hours was not nearly enough time to give her the support and encouragement needed to help sustain her peace of mind.

After our meeting, I could not sleep that night. The Lord woke me up at 2:08 am with a clear vision of what I was to do. I was to write this book and start a support group for pastor's wives. By 6:05 AM I had a clear outline and title for both.

It is extremely important for you to develop your own social network of pastor's wives to have a support system to lean on. If you know two to three other pastors or ministers wives you can start a group of your own. Even if you do not know any personally you may want to reach out to a few local pastors' wives and make new connections to form your group.

Here's How I Got Started:
Send an email or special hand written invitation:

SAMPLE
A pastor's wife is an ordinary woman in an extraordinary role. We all need encouraging words and a place to safely and **"honestly"** express our feelings about the various challenges that come with this position.

My Sister's Keeper is designed to be a place where pastor's wives can relax and enjoy the company of women whom we can identify with and understand each other like no one else can. We will laugh together, cry together, share our challenges, learn from one another and pray for each other. We won't have all the answers, but we can try to point each other in the right direction with the help of GOD and personal life experiences. Our mission is to help each other thrive instead of just survive in our "fishbowl" lives.

I would like to start out with a small, intimate group of ladies (8-10) so that we may get to know each other better.

This will be the founding group of **My Sister's Keeper** (Pastor's Wives Support Group). At our first gathering we will discuss how the meetings will best suit the needs of each woman, including future topics, formatting, meeting location(s) etc...

Now to the hard part.: How to clear eight to ten pastors' wives calendars on the same day. Please respond back and

Jeanne D. Wilson, Ed.D.

select the date that best fits your schedule. If you could manage either date just say available for all.

I look forward to developing a deeper relationship/friendship with you ladies for we are our Sisters Keeper! Romans 12:10.

My Sister's Keeper

Preparing to Host the Event:

Hold the meeting in an intimate setting, preferably your home and not the church. In your living or dining room make sure that seating arrangements are in a circle. Serve light refreshments. For a special touch you may even want to present your guest with a *Pastor's Wife Survival Kit* at the end of your gathering.

Kit Includes:

A small gift bag & a mini typed note that says what the contents of the bag are for.

Hand sanitizer-Lord knows we don't have time to be sick.

Gum & mints-To freshen the breath before greeting the members.

Hershey's kisses-For those moments we need to encourage ourselves....with chocolate. ☺

Hallmark card-To remind him how much you still love and support him.

How to Jump Start the Discussion

Read the following vignette out loud and then open the floor for discussion. After a brief discussion have each woman answer each question at the bottom of the page and then discuss as a group again.

Jeanne D. Wilson, Ed.D.

Shelia shifted uncomfortably in her 2nd row seat, fully aware that many eyes were watching her every move during service. She kept her expression blank with a hint of a smile on her face. Her eyes straight ahead but her mind thinks about events that occurred previous to this Sunday. Miles, her husband and the pastor, had been irritable and non-commutative yesterday, spending several hours working on a sermon. Shelia remembered that she needed to greet the two new members that joined after Bible study on Wednesday and she feels a little guilt for being snappy when Alicia called, again, for a loan because she got a 3-day notice from PG&E. Got to make sure to smooth those ruffled feathers.

Umm, Rev. Davis seems to be giving a mini-sermon when he should be giving a short prayer. Shelia made a mental note to let her husband Miles know that members do not like this. Sis. King comes by and pats her bare leg one more time! "Miles did not think this skirt was too short so why is she trying to regulate???? And, no, I don't have to wear white each 1st Sunday!!!!"

Miles is trying to move in a different direction in ministry but of course they smile in his face and grumble to Shelia. There goes Sis. Keisha's snotty nose child, running around the church again. Shelia wonders, "Where is his mother or at least one of the Children's Ministry workers. They know that child is a distraction to Pastor!" Sis. Leslie hits a high note that brings Shelia back from her thoughts.

Like Shelia, many wives of leaders take on the challenges of their husband's positions. Regardless of whether she receives a personal call to ministry or not, she, by virtue of her wedding vows, is called to support her husband and his concerns. Ministry calls for spouse and family to be fully supportive of the church and its members. More than a job, Ministry becomes a way of life, spiritually, emotionally and socially.

Vignette Discussion Questions:

A. What are the three top challenges you face as a Pastor's wife?

B. How can these meetings or this fellowship best suit your needs as a Pastors' wife?

C. Name two or three future topics you would like to discuss:

Schedule the Next Meeting:

1. How often do we want to meet? (i.e. Once a month? Every other month)

2. Location(s). Pick a different house each time or one central location?

3. Food: Potluck or Host provides food?

4. Facilitator/Discussion Leader-Choose a different one for each meeting

Jeanne D. Wilson, Ed.D.

After the Meeting:

Send a follow up email thanking the attendees and remind them of the next meeting date and time.

SAMPLE Email

I really enjoyed and more importantly, was extremely blessed by our first **My Sister's Keeper** meeting! I learned from my sisters to keep my children away from Pastor on Sunday mornings because they can be a major distraction and source of irritation to him before service.

What a difference a slight change made. I did not allow my girls to go anywhere near my husband until it was time for us to pray before leaving for church. My house was peaceful on Sunday morning without my husband having to fuss at kids for not cleaning up or getting dressed fast enough. He seemed more relaxed and free that morning. God is Good! ☺

Our next meeting is on Saturday January 15th at 4:00 pm. Sis. Patrice is hosting and Sis. Sherri will be our facilitator. Thank you all for attending and I look forward to seeing you soon.

In your new support group, you may find a woman of God who will help lift your sprits when you are down and provide spiritual counsel when you encounter delicate situations. She will pray with you and stand in the gap and intercede for you. When you are frustrated and weak, the women in your support group can be a valuable source of collective prayers and lived experiences that will have a positive impact on your mental and spiritual well being.

Reflections

Can you think of three women you may or may not know personally, that you could approach to start a pastor's wives support group? What are their names?

_____

_____

_____

How do you think a monthly or bi-monthly support group could help you?

_____

_____

_____

What is Your Plan of Action?

_____

_____

_____

My Sister's Keeper

Be devoted to one another in brotherly love;
give preference to one another in honor
Romans 12:10

Jeanne D. Wilson, Ed.D.

Chapter Seventeen:
Practice Test: How Could YOU be Your Sister's Keeper?

DR. JEANNE WILSON

Now here's a test for you. It's your turn to put into practice some of the valuable information you have received from this book. The following is a true story from a letter submitted to me by a wife who is hurting and needs your spiritual and practical advice. Your counsel could help save her marriage and lead her to finding joy through her journey as the wife of a pastor.

As you read pray about what you would say as she begins to open up and share how she really feels about being married to a pastor.

"Phillip and I just celebrated our sixth year anniversary in ministry. If anyone would ever ask me, "What advice would you give your daughter if she told you she was going to marry a Pastor?" I would say, "RUN! Run hard! Run fast! Run far, far away and don't look back or else you'll turn into a pillar of salt, or in my case into a rock of bitter salt.

I don't enjoy ministry. In fact, I've told Phillip that I feel absolutely no joy from the ministry. It drains me.

I go through the motions, but my heart is not in it. I get so angry sometimes, wondering, "Lord, what did I do to deserve this?

My Sister's Keeper

I hate sheep and sometimes even the shepherd. Well I guess I really don't *hate* them but I do have a strong dislike! Sheep are stubborn. Sheep are needy. Sheep are weak. Sheep look all soft and cute but when you get close; their wool is actually kind of hard, dirty and ugly! That describes a lot of our "flock" at the church (Sorry! I'm just keepin' it real). Some of those folks are just stubborn and stuck in tradition. They don't like change of any kind and are not open to new ideas.

Other folks are just needy. They want to call you all the time, schedule meetings, send emails and texts. They are in crisis, always crying-They just drain the life out of you! Others are just weak. You pour yourself, your time, your teaching into them and they go right back to doing what they were doing before you began ministering to them. Very few sheep actually bring glimmers of happiness and hope but then again, I guess that's not a sheep's role.

Okay, now let's get to "the shepherd" (Pastor). Notice I didn't say "THE SHEPHERD" (Lord and Savior). The one I'm talking about is my husband/Pastor/Phillip. Do I really need to elaborate on why he gets on my nerves? You're married, so you must have some idea.

Imagine being a referee several times a week. Your husband shoots off at the mouth but do the sheep go to him to cry and grumble? Noooooo. They come to you! You know your husband is wrong, but you can't say that so your next role is that of a tightrope walker. You have to balance on a fine line of pacifying the sheep without badmouthing the shepherd. You have to defend the shepherd but comfort the sheep. AUUUGGHHH!

Jeanne D. Wilson, Ed.D.

I'm employed full time outside the home, add in ministry and it feels like I have two full time jobs. When I'm at my job trying to give my employer the full 40 hours a week of work that they are paying me to do, don't think I won't get a text message, phone call, email, or even a personal visit *at my job* regarding church matters. Imagine being on call 24/7 to an entire congregation of the sheep. I have to solve folks problems, stop folks from fighting, comfort the sad, problem solve for the weak. Now do you see why I would say RUN?!?

And that's not all. I'm expected to go to every family funeral---even their fourth cousin once removed. I'm expected to be at every baby shower, birthday party, retirement party, anniversary party, graduation and on top of all that; I am expected to be at church every time the doors open. It can be so overwhelming.

Of course I could go on and on complaining about ministry, but I know that does not glorify God.

Hopefully, one day if my daughter were to marry a pastor, I could tell her *Sheep are Great and so is Being Married to a Shepherd*. But, I'm not there yet."

Reflections:

What "spiritual" advice would you give to your sister in Christ? Provide three scriptures that could comfort and guide her.

_____

_____

_____

What "practical" advice would you give to your sister in Christ that could comfort and guide her?

_____

_____

_____

Plan of Action:
What could you suggest that she do? (Hint: My Sister's Keeper Support Group)

_____

_____

_____

Jeanne D. Wilson, Ed.D.

I am purposely not providing "answers" to this test because there is no cookie cutter prescription to all problems. God has given each of us individual and unique ways of ministering to others, so whatever answers HE directed you to give to a sister in need of counsel deserves an "A+".

It is my sincere desire that this book has helped you my sister in Christ, to accept and embrace the opportunity and gift God has given you to serve in ministry with your husband.

Mary McCloud Bethune said, "Let each one teach one." I thank each woman who "taught" us by sharing her personal experience and for being transparent about her life in order to impart spiritual guidance, godly wisdom and practical advice for other pastors' wives.

May your marriages and ministries be blessed beyond measure because of these letters from the Hearts of your Sister's Keepers.

TO CONTACT THE AUTHOR:

Dr. Jeanne D. Wilson

Revelation Christian Fellowship
1670 Orchard Ave
San Leandro, CA 94577

(510) 352-4707
DrJeanneWilson@aol.com